HUE COLORING

Focus on the Positive
Adult Coloring Book

IN THIS COLORING BOOK...

50 Positive Coloring Designs are included in this adult coloring book to help you relax and make your life more colorful. These illustrations are created for you to bring enjoyment to your life, and designed with beautiful patterns that appeal to adult eyes.

TIPS TO A FUN COLORING

Find a quiet space. It's easier to focus on what you are doing when there are no distractions.

Organize your materials. Lay out your coloring book and crayons, pens, or pencils.

Set the mood. Turn on some tranquil music, diffuse lavender or another relaxing oil, and make sure you have your preferred drink at hand.

Select your picture. Which image speaks to you today? That's the one you should color. Choose your palette. Select the colors you will be using for your image.

Begin coloring. This is the fun part. Don't worry about getting everything perfect; just start. If you feel you don't want to do it anymore, just stop!

SHOW US YOUR CREATION!

We'd love to hear from you, show us what you created.
Facebook: www.facebook.com/huecoloring
Pinterest: www.pinterest.com/huecoloring
Please be sure to subscribe to our newsletter by visiting: huecoloring.com. We'll show you our latest coloring projects as well as giving you information of the best deals.

Focus on
the positive

Stay focused on
your Creativity

No rain,
No flowers

Two hearts
in love need
no words

Above all else, guard your heart,
for everything you do flows from it.

Simple
but
effective

Live What You Love

a little progress
each day leads
to a great result.

LIFE
IS A
GIFT

People Who
Are Crazy
Enough To
Think They
Can Change
The World,
Are The Ones
Who Do

Stop
AND
Smell
THE
flowers

Be kind. Be mindful. Be grateful. Be positive. Be true.

Love yourself

Attitude is a little thing
that makes a big difference.

Be the change that you wish to see in the world.

Do stuff. Be clenched, curious. Not Waiting for inspiration's shove or society's kiss on your forehead. Pay attention. It's all about paying attention. Attention is vitality. It connects you with others. It makes you eager. Stay eager...

Shoot for the moon,
You might get there.

Love
There is only one happiness in this life, to love and be loved..

THE
GREATEST
HEALING
THERAPY
IS
FRIENDSHIP
AND
LOVE.

Be free, and happy

Live
Your
Dream

Good things
take time

The two most important days
are the day you are born
and they day you find out why

Follow
your
heart

Keep going.
Live.
Begin.
Breathe.
Enjoy.
Go for it.

We
Rise By
Lifting
others

You are a work of art

Focus
on the
good

You are amazing. Remember that.

Every
moment
matters

Happiness
looks
gorgeous
on you.

Life can only be understood backwards.

START YOUR
morning
with a
SMILE

Whatever you do,
do with all your might.

Once you have tasted flight, you will forever
walk the earth with your eyes turned skyward

WHEREVER LIFE PLANTS YOU, BLOOM WITH GRACE

Let
the
sea
set
you
free

Escape
the
Ordinary

Rest
and be
thankful.

WHEREVER FLOWERS BLOOM
SO DOES HOPE

Begin
Today

All good
things
are wild
and free.

SEE
THE
GOOD

today
is
going
to be
a
Great
Day

We
Become
What We
Think About

Look on the
Brightside

Love is the flower you've got to let grow

I prefer being a small
fish in a big pond

Friendship is
A sheltering tree

BE your
own HERO